FALLEN
FAITH
HOPE

Ms. D

WestBow
PRESS

WestBow Press books may be ordered through booksellers or by contacting:

WestBow Press
A Division of Thomas Nelson
1663 Liberty Drive
Bloomington, IN 47403
www.westbowpress.com
1-(866) 928-1240

ISBN: 978-1-4497-0147-5 (sc)
ISBN: 978-1-4497-0155-0 (hc)
ISBN: 978-1-4497-0146-8 (e)

Library of Congress Control Number: 2010926343

Printed in the United States of America

WestBow Press rev. date: 04/21/2010

This book is dedicated to God Almighty, to education, to life experiences, and to all the souls it may help come to the Lord.

Contents

Acknowledgments

Sincere thanks to my godparents for teaching and living the truth, for their encouragement and support, and for being who they claim to be. Thanks also to family, friends, and associates for the life experiences. Finally, the utmost thanks to God for bringing me out of spiritual bondage.

Introduction

I, Ms. D, am a God-fearing woman of the United States who was inspired by God's word to write this book in order to help all who will take heed and receive truth as spoken through poetry. Acting on this inspiration is long overdue. I thank God for his ultimate love, Jesus, who gave me the determination to never give up. The poems here may or may not apply to you personally, but you may know someone who might be helped by them. The poems in this book may describe what you, your loved ones, friends, or foes are doing right—or wrong—according to the Bible. I've also provided a place for you to take notes or record your own thoughts.

Testimony

"Greater love hath no man than this, that a man lay down his life for his friends" (John 15:13 KJV). God wants us to sacrifice our time to help others, and that is what I am doing with this book. Hopefully my readers will enjoy the messages and use the poetry to help others. Here is one of my miraculous testimonies:

In about 2002, I was diagnosed with an illness called lupus that is incurable, according to doctors. Lupus affects the immune system. It can rob you of your ability to walk, talk, and see clearly, and eventually it destroys your ability to care for yourself. Eventually your personal freedom is totally gone. This is what lupus did to me.

I was extremely sensitive to light to the point that any amount of daylight burned my skin. My children and I lived in a slightly darkened apartment unless I had on long sleeved shirts, a pair of pants, long socks, and something to protect my face and hands from light exposure. Going outside required even more precautions. Self-pity hit, and I felt totally worthless, like a vagabond on the earth who couldn't be helped, wouldn't be helped, or shouldn't be helped because of past sins against God's will.

At times my joints locked in whatever position I was in at the time. Excruciating pain followed, and if I happened to be standing up when it happened, I fell face first onto the ground. Eventually my strength failed. I couldn't hold on to anything that weighed more than two pounds. Not only did I have to give up playing sports and games with my children, I could no longer do their hair, cook for them, take them to the park, clean the house, do laundry, visit school, or go to church. I was completely housebound.

By August 2002 I could no longer take care of myself, clean the house, do laundry, talk, or go to church. I was completely housebound. I was terrified that I would lose my children, so I began to pray. God answered me after several prayers. He sent help in the guise of strangers who offered their act of charity. They cooked, cleaned, shopped for groceries, and tried to make me laugh. I remember crying and pleading unto God to take the lupus away. I felt like I had failed my children. I needed God to provide a breakthrough.

Nothing happened until February 2003 when I pleaded with God to provide me with a home Bible study; again in my mind. I thought God had provided me with the home Bible study I truly desired. I wasn't specific in my request of God for a true home Bible study, so I was provided with greeting visitations and desserts on a monthly basis. The person who was to do the home Bible study would come to my home without a Bible or study materials; asked how I was doing; bring some desserts; and then tell me that she would see me next month. I got so frustrated. All kinds of thoughts were running through my mind at this time. The first one was, "What kind of home Bible study is this"? I continued to plead with God to provide true home Bible study.

In late April of 2003, God bless me with a true home Bible study. He sent a husband and wife from a church I eventually joined who read the Bible to me, explained the Bible to me, and encouraged me to keep working on talking to receive my speech back. You better believe I was full of so much joy, and I became so determined to talk that God gave me back my my ability to verbally talk, sing, yell, hum, and praise.

In early May of that year, my mobility returned. I was so grateful to once again be able to take a walk with my children. As I continued in Bible study, God continued to bless me. My strength returned. The more I read, lived, and told others about God's word, the more my limitations faded away. Hallelujah! Praise be to God! I can now walk, talk, see without glasses, run, clean my home, and provide for my children. I continue to read, teach, and live God's will.

In February of 2006, I had routine blood work done. The result was negative. The doctors were telling me I needed to come back for more blood work in several months. I went back and got that blood work done. The results were still negative. The doctor tried to tell me to still take the medicine. I refused. No more locked joint! I thank God for choosing me as one of his elect to be about his business. It is truly a privilege. May God bless you through this testimony, his word, and the following poems.

FALLEN

∽

The fallen have disobeyed
God's will (have sinned).

What Is Conviction and Who Is Convicting You?

❧

John 16:8–11; II Peter 2:4–10; Matthew 8:12; Proverbs 3:1–2, 10:27

Conviction in the natural sense is being found guilty of and charged with a crime by earth's judiciary system.

Conviction in the spiritual sense is the judgment of God toward:

- those who do not believe in him (God, Jesus, and the Holy Spirit are the creators of all and control everything);
- those who won't accept the truth for what it is (Jesus came, died for all sins, and rose from the dead. He is the savior of all);
- those with the spirit of the devil who must do wrong to feel good and who make excuses for that wrong. Such convictions lead to the ultimate judgment of being left as the devil's plaything, whether alive or dead.

When a person won't accept the conviction of God, he or she won't accept forgiveness, either. May these poems help you to understand that you are damaging your soul when they do not accept the love of God.

Notes

_____

_____

_____

_____

_____

Convicted by God's Spirit

It's not the person speaking,
It's the Holy Spirit within,
Who gives a person a message
From God to mankind to send.

So please don't revile against him;
You are reviling against the Spirit of God.
Also against his word,
That helps you live long.

You are being convicted by God's Spirit.

When One Will Not Accept Forgiveness Given

You truly hurt someone's feelings that Sunday afternoon;
You treated them as vultures coming for your bloom.
They did not want to come, the spirit lets them know how you feel;
Fellowship with them … you could not deal.
Because of something you have done some time ago,
Please! Leave it alone. Let it go.

Your forgiveness unknowingly was already done;
Before you came back to Christ
Your forgiveness you've won.
Please stop dwelling … let it roll;
You're messing up your peace of mind; so let it go.

Hopefully, someday, your blindness turns into sight;
Let it be that weeping only endureth for a night.
Please stop dwelling … let it roll;
You're messing up your soul; so let it go.

What Causes You to Be Convicted?

⌒

Proverbs 3:5–8, 17:4–5, 17:9–11; Exodus 20:3–17; Galatians 5:19–21; Romans 12:19; Isaiah 13:11; Revelations 21:7; John 13:34

Conviction comes to people who live life according to their own understanding instead of living the way God would have them live. They believe it is okay to do wrong. Some people believe that vengeance is okay. That is not so.

What is wrongdoing according to God? It is actions and thoughts that go against the Ten Commandments and any other commandment given in the Bible. Jealousy, coveting, murdering, causing divisions, sorcery, hatred, arguing, antagonizing, deceitfulness, unfaithfulness, and self-righteousness are all works of the flesh and come from evil spirits. Deceitfulness is a spirit that lays in wait to reveal his wickedness to the one he has deceived.

May the following poems help readers to understand how God truly abhors wickedness, no matter what form it takes.

Notes

_____

_____

_____

_____

_____

_____

_____

_____

Works of the Flesh

The works of the flesh, they are not good.
By God's will, you are not to do
Adultery, fornication, uncleanness, and lasciviousness;
Idolatry, witchcraft, hatred, and variance.

The works of the flesh, they are not good.
By God's will, you are not to do
Emulations, wrath, strife, seditions, and heresies;
Envyings, murders, drunkenness, and revellings.

The works of the flesh, they are not good.
By God's will, you are not to do.
Should you not obey what the Lord's will is?
Surely you can not be any of his.

Witnessing to Someone: Not Knowing Their Ultimate Plan

❧

You know that everything that I have said to you is the truth.
You tried to be vindictive,
For your family to give attention to you
You have not done anything but
Break whatever good spirit you had within.
You chose reviling, wrath, and strife. Those are sins.

You say that I have deceived you. No, you are truly wrong.
You used me to seek self-pity
While your wickedness still prolongs.
You thought that I would be scared of what you had to say
Because you brought your family.
No, my dictation stayed the same.

I just pray that you learn a better way to live your life
Because it's surely *not* revile, wrath, or strife.

Where Do Evil Spirits Come From and Who Are You Working For?

❧

John 3:16, 8:44, 10:10; I John 3:8; Proverbs 16:27–31, 20:22; Revelations 12:9; I Thessalonians 5:15; I Peter 3:9; Deuteronomy 32:9;

Bad behaviors derive from evil spirits. These evil spirits are of the antichrist (the devil). When people allow these spirits to influence them to do the wrong things, they are working for the devil. According to the Bible, no one is to render evil for evil because Jesus died and paid for all our sins. God will justify you in due time because vengeance is his. The antichrist is not Jesus and cannot ever be Jesus, but he has sometimes deceived people into believing he is Jesus. God has only one Son. That Son is the Lord and Savior, Jesus Christ.

Notes

_____

_____

_____

_____

_____

_____

_____

_____

_____

_____

_____

Antichrist

He is a liar, a cheater, a destroyer, and a deceiver.
He is wicked and envious.
He is bitterness, hatred, and unrighteousness.

Antichrist is not Jesus. He is the devil.
Do not believe in, worship, or idolize him,
Or the truth in you will shrivel

Because he deceives you, and hinders you
But will never love you.

Don't Be Deceived

Jesus is not he who wishes to deceive.
It's the devil that fills you with envy.
He comes to consume your mind so you'll be blind.
If you allow him to, you could run out of time.
The antichrist is here; he has not been revealed.
So call on Jesus Christ, and live in his true will.

What Happens When One Does Wrong; What Is It Called? What to Do?

༄

Proverbs 29:22–27; Ephesians 4:30–5:1-21; John 3:16; II Chronicles 7:14; Romans 1:3–6; Matthew 11:28, 18:11

Naturally, when people do something wrong they are judged by the people. Sometimes people in the wrong will not have any remorse until they are caught in action or lose something they love because of it. Unremorseful people are full of resentment and anger. Resentment and despising anger cause people to reject goodness and sometimes seek revenge. These are dangerous spirits that can lead to total destruction of people's lives and make their road to recovery very strenuous.

Spiritually, when people do something wrong they are judged by the word, lifestyle, and laws of God. Those who do not seek to get themselves right with God (won't repent) but still proclaim to be saved have committed spiritual adultery.

Spiritual adultery occurs when a person claims to have faith in God, the Son, and the Holy Spirit only to receive glory unto himself instead of God. The person acts as if he or she knows everything and will believe a delusion over the truth. Arrogance, lies, and undermining spirits cause one to lose the glory, hope, joy, and peace of the Lord. Doing so, the person has left an open door for the devil to intrude upon their heart, mind, body, and soul.

Once believers have committed a sin, they need to come back unto Jesus at the altar and start all over again. Jesus said for all to come unto him.

Notes

_____

_____

_____

Despising Anger

The feeling of hatred flows right through
Continues on until you lose your cool

You want to hit, hold back, and get sick
All of a sudden, your mind clicks …

You let out your anger, you let it out strong
Thinking because you didn't hit, you would not be wrong.

Thinking of a plan to hurt a person
Don't realize it's you and God you're hurting

Your anger is so strong, and you don't even care
Desiring this person to be in despair

Because favor of God that shows in their life
You planned and schemed to bring them strife
Failed to realize your actions are being recorded
By family, friends, foes, you name it … they're doing it

Most importantly, you're recorded by God
Please repent of your sin and don't be a fraud

Now that you know what this Spirit is for
Please don't go back and give Satan this door

Just rejoice in the Lord forevermore
For forgiving you of your sins and the Spirit he pours

Road to Recovery

꩜

Bound by drugs and alcohol,
Your motivation was a destructible call.
Satan kept promising you so much
But all you needed was Jesus' touch.
You ignored God's call unto you,
So proclamation of Satan you were given to.

After many days, months, and years of torment
By the ruler of all evil you decide to live on.
You started praising and worshipping God.
Suddenly, a light came on.
You were so low in your heart,
All you could do was cry.
Praying unto God, saying, "Please do not pass me by!"
He answered with his grace and mercy
By lifting your burdens and making you new.
You had to make a choice,
And did you choose.

Thank God you chose Jesus,
Now your heart is filled with joy.
Consistently having Jesus on your mind,
The Holy Spirit kept you from all decoys.

Your road to recovery
May have taken a long time,
But you kept seeking, praying, and worshiping God,
Where the Lord can say, "You are now mine."

So stay in righteousness, and be fervent in prayers.
The Holy Ghost will build you up in many layers.
Oh yes, the enemy is coming back.
The difference is the Holy Ghost is what it lacks.

Does it not feel so glorious in this way?
Don't look back, just get on your knees and pray.
So do not worry about the things you used to do.
For the Spirit of God is protecting you.
Road to Recovery …

Spiritual Adultery

Worthless faith, vain glory;
Spiritual adultery is this story.

Impure heart …
So you have fallen.
You're no longer soaring
Like a falcon.

Diluted illusions …
Satan's open door.
Heart intruded;
He stole your joy.

Idolatry …
Praise given higher than God
Enemy influence;
You became a fraud.

Inward or outwardly …
This is spiritual adultery.

Jesus is Calling You

Jesus said, "Come unto me;
I broke the chains to set you free.
I took the key of death, hell, and the grave.
For the ransom of your life, I am the way.
For you to reach the Almighty God
The only true living and he's no fraud.
I'll take your plea unto the Father.
As long as it is me you're coming after.
Deny yourself, come unto me.
Because I am the mediator between you and thee."
Jesus is calling you ...

What Is Repentance? How Do You Do It? Why Are You Asking?

John 14:6; Psalms 51, 111:10

Repentance happens when people recognize what they have done wrong, regret that they have done it, and ask God to forgive them of their sins through Jesus Christ. With that regret, people must change their ways to prove their repentance was true.

Jesus is the one who forgives you of your sins. He's the only way for you to reach God.

The natural reason for asking for forgiveness is to get rid of the guilt and shame at that time. The true reason to repent is so that your name will be written in the Book of Life. This means that should you die at the moment of repentance, you're going to heaven when Jesus comes back to earth for his people. It does not matter who you are, what title you hold, or what good deed you have done in the past. God is no respecter of persons. We all need to repent.

When you're truly tired of the enemy oppressing you, you will repent and thank God for your freedom through Christ Jesus. You can only do so by surrendering your all to Jesus and being made whole.

Now is the time to make a decision on where your soul will lie. All it takes is repentance from the heart; asking God to cleanse your soul by healing your heart, mind, body, and the spirit that lies within you.

Notes

_____

_____

_____

Decision Time

Live in the present, not in the past.
If you dwell on the past, you'll lose your liveliness fast.
Past wrongdoings come to keep you bound in sin.
As long as you dwell on them, you can not win.

They enemy reminds you of your sins, to seek or keep control.
If you allow him to, your soul will be waxed cold.

Repent of your sins, and be baptized.
Do not wait, because now may be your last time
To give the Lord your soul, mind, and heart.
Do not forget him, or from you he will depart.

Thank God for the breath of life.
For Jesus died for us all to have a chance
To be written in the Book of Life.

So Surrender Your All to Jesus and Be Made Whole

Let the Spirit of the Lord guide you in every thought
Let the Spirit of the Lord fulfill your heart
Let the Spirit of the Lord show you his love
Let the Spirit of the Lord be the reason for soaring above
Let the Spirit of the Lord give you the words to speak
Let the Spirit of the Lord keep you meek
Let the Spirit of the Lord uplift your woes
So surrender your all to Jesus and be made whole.

As you surrender your all to Jesus and be made whole
Your life will shine more than silver and gold
Tell the Lord's word to all nations as we all are told
By the Holy Bible, which is the truth that is strong and bold.

Cleansing the Heart

Create in me a loving heart
To dwell in your will
And never set me apart

Cleanse me, O Lord
Purify my soul
I'm sorry for my sins
I don't want to be frozen

Redeem me, O Lord
My heart has been trodden
I am confessing
That I have not forgotten

Restore me, O Lord
Please return my joy
I am tired of Satan
Having me as his toy

Thank you, O Lord
I am no longer oppressed
It's in you, dear Jesus
My life shall I rest

How Believers Lose the Holy Spirit's Covering and What to Do About It.

⌒

Proverbs 3: 5–6; Psalms 97:7; Matthew 7:15, 10:28; Jeremiah 14:14–15, 15:6–7; Revelations 21:7; Romans 12:9; Deuteronomy 31:6; Galatians 5:22–23, 6:7-8

When people live according to their own understanding, they believe a lie and are damned. Satan gave Eve a diluted illusion in the book of Genesis. Read what happened to her. People even brought forth their own images to brag about themselves instead of thanking God for the blessing; which they find themselves confused. Read what happen to the people who were building the tower of Babel in the 11th chapter of Genesis. God will not be mocked. Just as quick as people are blessed by God, they can lose their blessings. Sometimes people blame everybody but themselves for the choices they have made. Deception is the enemy's only tool.

Remember to be strong and resist the devil while going through your tests and persecutions, and know that Jesus can send the spirits of the devil back to hell (the devil's home), from where they came. As you do so, you have gone from being a sinner to a Christian, striving to make it to the Promised Land (heaven).

Notes

_____

_____

_____

_____

_____

_____

How One Loses the Fruits of the Spirit

False hopes, false prophets;
This is how you lost them.
Love, joy, and peace;
Because you've been deceived.
Longsuffering and gentleness;
Because of the wickedness.
Goodness and faith
Because of choices you've made.
Meekness and temperance
Because you lost your deliverance.
No reason to blame anyone else;
You made those decisions; you … yourself.

Be Strong!

Mislead and deceived by someone *close* to you,
For the enemy within them caused you to be confused.
Depression and temptations were close on their way,
You shouted, "Thank you, Jesus, through your will I can pray!"
Yes, maybe you were struggling for your spirit to be renewed.
In the mist of it all, the enemy did not have a clue.

The Lord dwells in you, more than you or the enemy knows.
Until you both see, the Spirit of the fiery Holy Ghost.
The enemy is now angry, mad in rage.
He had to flee back into his cage,
Where he plans to scheme on his next attack;
Don't worry. Jesus has his own plans to send Satan right back.

The enemy cannot be right in anything he does.
He does not believe in unconditional love.
Continue to pray with all your might;
Because every day of life is a spiritual fight.

Sinner to Christian to the Promised Land

All the sadness in your life can be rushed away
And you will no longer blue
All the rumors and corrupt lifestyles will have no say
That people won't have a clue

Oh yes! They will try to run you dry
Of your senses of humanity
Have the proclivity
Attempt to defile your dignity
Without any sensitivity

So just call on Jesus and pray unto his holy name
You will be able to shout, "Hallelujah … I'm saved!"

See, Jesus Christ is your only way
Into Heaven
Not by good deeds, nor through marriage,
And definitely not the lucky sevens

Only by following Jesus' commandments
And having true faith in him
You will be where the light is bright
I'm confident that it surely will not be dim

You faithfully abide by the commandments
And now you're in the Book of Life
Please don't backslide, or seven more demonic spirits
On your back will bring you grief and strife

Satan has no mercy, but he leads people to believe so
Again, faithfully call on Jesus and Satan will have to go

You continue to faithfully live the life of the Lord
Hallelujah, you are in the Promised Land, shouting,
"Joy forever more!"

That lets you know
The Lord's words are true;
Seek him first and the kingdom of God
And the rest shall be added unto you

FAITH

∽

*Faith is believing and trusting you will
receive something through Jesus Christ
by the power of God without seeing
that something before your eyes.*

What Are the Perceptions of Faith?

Hebrews 11:1, 6; Psalms 118:8; I Corinthians 2:5, 14:33; Romans 3:3–4, 10:17, 11:20–23; Proverbs 3:5–8; Matthew 6:33; John 1:1–14; Galatians 4:4, 6:7–8; Philippians 2:6–11; I Timothy 3:16

Naturally, the faith of mankind leads humans to believe that they will receive something through their own power. Some people believe that it was their faith in God that got them the desires of their heart, when in fact they had used undermining, degrading, deceiving, and coveting spirits and actions to achieve those desires. Not so. The bible says in

Galatians 6:7–8, "Be not deceived; God is not mocked: for whatsoever a man soweth, that shall he also reap. For he that soweth to his flesh shall of the flesh reap corruption; but he that soweth to the Spirit shall of the Spirit reap life everlasting."

Spiritually, the faith of mankind is believing and trusting in receiving something through Jesus Christ by the power of God without seeing that something before your eyes. This means mankind must trust and believe without a doubt that God will give them the desires of their hearts. Spiritual faith comes from no other than God through Christ Jesus, meaning that all must recognize and believe who God the Father, the Son, and the Holy Ghost really are and shut down their own will (understanding).

Notes

_____

_____

_____

_____

_____

Recognizing God

God is almighty
He overcomes all things
He sent his beloved Son
Over us all he reigns
Jesus was scourged for all souls
Not just mine
Every day and every hour
Is God's time
Hallelujah, thank God for being saved
Because he deserves all glory, honor, and praise.

God as the Son

God is with us;
Who can be against us?
He sent Jesus in flesh form;

Who came to live among us,
In righteousness he came to teach us,
And performed miracles as proof that he's the balm.

Jesus that taught God's will to us,
When Satan comes to tempt us,
Jesus is who we shall call upon.

He is the only one who can save us;
He will not ever leave us
As long as our understanding is not of our own.

Jesus owns all of us;
In him we shall trust,
So please repent to Jesus, and get reborn.

God is with us;
Who can be against us?
He sent Jesus in flesh form.

Jesus is the Light

Jesus is the light both day and night;
He evaporates wickedness and knocks it out of sight

Sin is gone and Jesus saved your soul;
Thank God your soul was not waxed cold

Hallelujah, give the Lord the highest praise
For using you in his will in various ways.

Read, study, and teach his will with compassion;
Talk, walk, and live in his will with such profession.

John the Baptist confirmed the light in John 1:7
And spoke how Jesus would lead men into heaven.

Jesus brought you to the light because of his love,
The love which descended from up above.

Deities of Jesus

Jesus is of the Father, Son, and Holy Ghost
They work together as one; they're the Lord of Host
He's our guider, provider, and warrior.
He's our maker, healer, and Savior.

Jesus is love, peace, kind, and holy.
He is gentle, grace, mercy, and the Hope of Glory.
He is the answer to all, any, and everything,
Just as long as you submit yourself under his wings.

Jesus is of the Father, Son, and Holy Ghost
They work together as one; they're the Lord of Host
He's our guider, provider, and warrior.
He's our maker, healer, and Savior.
Deities of Jesus …

Jesus Is

He's the Savior of all souls;
He paid for all sins, young and old;
He's the protector from all evil deeds;
As long as on him you lean;
Jesus Is …

He's the counselor and comforter through all things;
Leaning on him, you will have peace;
He's the provider of all needs;
Have faith in him, at the size of a mustard seed;
Your needs, you shall receive;
Jesus Is …

He's the one full of grace and mercy;
When you repent from the heart unto thee;
Unique is he; there is none like thee;
To break the chains and set all souls free;
He's of the Alpha and Omega; he's a deity;
Jesus Is …

Recognizing Self-will Doesn't Work

∽

Thank you, Jesus, for your ways; they're here to help us all
You gave your life for all our sins so that we may hear God's call

To live the life of peace and mercy
Just as God has given to you
Loving one another at all times,
You said, "Treat others as you would have them to do unto you"

Your word taught us how to love and be grateful
No matter where we're at
Because what is done is done; we cannot change it
By keeping on looking back

We're to press forward to the prize of our high calling
Of God that is in you
By surrendering our all, O Lord our Savior, as you command us to
So then the Father, God Almighty, would graciously approve
And say unto all his children, "I am well pleased with you."

Giving God the praise everyday no matter where we stand
It does not matter if you're a boy or girl, a man or woman
He has no respect of persons as you can tell
All that's needed for us to do is shut down our own will.

How Can You Increase Your Faith?

∾

Romans 10:17; Galatians 3:2, 5; Hebrews 10:23–26; Ephesians 4:11–32; John 14:6; Luke 18:18–19

Naturally minded, you would not want to increase your faith. Natural faith is of self-will. Self-will is tied into selfishness. Good deeds done in self-will are done to praise oneself than to pass or give all glory unto God. All good is of God.

Believers can increase their faith in God by hearing his word. This means believers trust and believe in God because of what they have heard about Jesus Christ. Believers also keep themselves among other saints to help encourage them further in their walk with God. For this cause, Jesus appointed apostles, prophets, evangelists, pastors, and teachers of the ministry. Therefore, believers must find themselves in the house of God as well as recognize their constant need of him through Jesus. Such recognition causes believers to identify life as a spiritual fight for hope.

Notes

_____

_____

_____

_____

_____

_____

_____

_____

_____

_____

Daily Bread

The word of God
Needs to be read;
"Build your spirits,"
The Holy Bible said;
Powerful laws
Must be obeyed;
The truth of life,
It does not play;
The strength to cope;
That gives you hope;
Save our souls,
We're going home.

Word of God

Hold it dear
Hold it close
Everyone needs it
To thee uttermost

Read it loud or quietly
Just make sure that
You take heed

Should you not
Understand
Let a man of God
Tell God's great plan
Why Jesus died
For you and me;
For our souls to live with
The Hope of Glory

Thank You, Trinity

Thank you, Jesus, for hearing my cry
And sending them unto God
Thank you, dear God Almighty,
For being who you are

Thank you, Jesus, for paying the ransom
For sins of any kind
Without your love and obedience to God
Spirit and truth I could not find

Thank you, God, for the Holy Ghost
It is the perfect guide
It provides me with joy, health, and strength
Which brings forth life

To help keep us from the enemy
Who is nothing but a lie
This is why I hold on to your Son
To receive everlasting life

Recognizing the Need of God

I surrender my all to the Almighty God
Thanking him for the escapes from the wicked rods
Satan is a lie, and he bares no truth
I thank you, Lord, for your approval
I love you, Lord, with all my heart
Demonic spirits, I must stay apart
I deny myself each and every day
Your love, O God, I cannot explain
The joy it brings the tears that fall
The well of salvation craved from the heart
The smiles it brings and the correction that comes
Only because you want me to make it to heaven
I cannot make it living on my own will
I must continue to surrender all and peace will be still
No matter where I go or where my life may lead
I must continue to surrender all for you to stay within me
I need your strength, wisdom, and courage to be bold
In order to speak of the greatest story ever told
God, I recognize that you are in control

Recognizing Life as a Spiritual Fight

Life is a spiritual battlefield
It's all about your will to live
Living in righteousness is what I am talking about
There's no need for arrogance ... cast the devil out
The devil is a murder, robber, and a thief
He is so busy trying to be the chief
The only true chief is Almighty God
Satan was thrown from heaven because he was proud
So now he's trying to get all that he can
Devouring souls is his demonic plan
Continue to read God's word, fast, and pray
The Spirit of God will send the enemy on his way
Hallelujah! Thank God for the spiritual fight
Because in the end, you will have peace and joy both day and night

HOPE

Hope is believing that God will give you the strength to overcome all things that will come against you for Jesus' name's sake.

What Are the Perceptions of Hope?

∽

Romans 15:13, 12:12; Luke 11:1, 18:1, 21:19; Isaiah 55:1; John 14:6; Psalms 130:5; Lamentations 3:24–25; Isaiah 30:18; Matthew 21:21–22; James 5:15; Acts 6:4; I Thessalonians 5:17; II Timothy 2:5

Naturally minded, hope is expecting something to happen through men because of their own actions taken to receive that something (they feel as if the something is owed to them). There are people who hope for those things to happen because of what they have done instead of how they did it. If you compete for any position, privileges, or award, you are to compete righteously or there is no truth in your position.

Spiritually minded, hope is an act of believing and trusting God's will to give you the strength to overcome all things that come against you for Jesus' name's sake. This means you must wait on God to bring you out of your troubles and always find yourself fasting and praying (talking with God). Such actions please God and make the devil flee.

Hope is driven from the Spirit of the Holy Ghost. The Holy Ghost reveals the confidence that God will reward those who diligently seek him, which brings forth the well of salvation.

Notes

_____

_____

_____

_____

_____

_____

Always Prayer

If you're tired of being depressed
And seek rest from it
You need prayer.

If you know you or a loved one has done something wrong
And do not want it to prolong
You need prayer.

If your life has turned upside down
And you're tired of frowning
You need prayer.

I know a man
Who loves you more than anyone can
Why not have prayer?

If you don't know what to do
About what's required of you
Repent, make it right, and still find yourself in prayer.

My Faith and Hope in Jesus

I am healed by the stripes of Jesus,
Because he died for all sins at Calvary
Shed the blood that protects me;
It is full of his spirit that is all so sweet.

I am redeemed by the Holy Spirit of Jesus,
Because he uplifted my woes and gave me peace
And made me a stronger witness for thee
In hope of submissions to the Hope of Glory.

I am covered by the holy blood of Jesus,
Because he is the creator and the abider
The protector and the guider
He is the balm and the provider.

I am staying and keeping my walk with Jesus,
Because he is the counselor and the comforter
"In the name of Jesus, flee Lucifer!"
I live by the will of the Wonderful Counselor.

Jesus is the only way to salvation …

Well of Salvation

Heart depth, sobering prayers
Lift off burdens, "Alleluia!"

Repented and committed, you have done
For giving up evil, you have won.

Tears of waterfall
Flow so gloriously
Yes, Lord
Thank you for your mercy.

I will live by your will; your will alone
Your statues, Lord, I will obey and hone.

In Jesus' name I pray
Amen.

How Can You Increase in Hope?

Psalm 118:8; Philippians 3:3

Naturally minded people increase in hope falsely. They look for people to bring them hope instead of the Spirit revealed in the person. One must be careful, because he or she could become a puppet for people who spitefully use them to just disappoint or hurt them over and over again. This is why the word of God tells us, "It is better to trust in the Lord than to put our confidence in man."

Spiritually minded people can increase their hope by continually increasing their faith (study, tell, and live in the will of God), and by having an attitude of gratitude towards God by praising and worshipping him.

God deserves all glory.

Notes

_____

_____

_____

_____

_____

_____

_____

_____

_____

_____

Attitude of Gratitude Toward God

Yes, Lord, I will bless your name.
Hallelujah! I give you the highest praise.
Thank you, Lord, for all you have done.
Thank you, Lord, for the souls you have won.
I thank you, Lord, for your decree.
That is to bless others and me.

God, you said that I don't have to fight
Because you're my warrior both day and night.
Thank you for your peace.
I thank you for your grace.
Thank you for your love.
I seek to see your face.

Thank you, God, for your glory.
I will continue to tell your greatest story.

Glory unto God

All glory belong to God
Hear all, ye people
Find yourselves before his glory
As well as under the steeple

Crying out to God
Thanking him for forgiving you of your sins
Thanking him for his Son
Who broke the chains so you can enter in

Thanking him for the Holy Ghost
Who shall guide you in spirit and truth
God the Father … the creator
He is the root

Praise and Worship

Praise and worship
Is what all should do,
For God is always watching you.

Praise and worship
In a righteous way,
Thanking him for the spiritual day.

Give him all the glory, honor, and praise
For allowing you to wake up to this new day.

Your mind is free,
You're clapping your hands;
You're stomping your feet,
You may even dance;
You let out a sudden shout,
Letting all know who it's all about.

You sing a song,
You raise your hands;
You feel Jesus' touch
As you sit or stand;
You let out a sudden shout,
Letting all know who it's all about.

Give the highest praise
Unto Jesus' name;
For washing your sins
And deleting your shame;
You let out a sudden shout,
Letting all know who it's all about.

Submit your talents unto the Lord,
Thanking him for now and beyond;
Clapping your hands and leaping for joy
Because God kept you from all decoys;
Shouting as you uplift his name,
As the anointment pours, others do the same.

The Holy Spirit, contagious, you know;
It's a free flowing spirit and that gives off a glow.
The Fruits of the Spirit and the beatitudes too;
These are the blessings from God to you.
You let out a sudden shout,
Letting all know who it's all about.

Praise and worship
Is what all should do,
For God is always watching you.

Praise and worship
In a righteous way,
Thanking him for the spiritual day.

Give him all glory, honor, and praise
For allowing you to wake up to this new day.

What Should Believers Always Remember?

❧

II Timothy 1:12; Matthew 6:33, 7:7–8; II Timothy 2:8–3:7, 4:1–6; Romans 12:1; I Timothy 4:12; I Peter 5:7; Luke 10:19

Believers should always to remember in whom they believe. Jesus resurrected from the dead by the power of God. Therefore, present yourselves as children of God following after the example of Jesus Christ. Saints (believers) remember also whose name you shall call upon in your time of trouble or whatever you care about. Also, recognize that you have the power over all the power of the enemy. God will defend you.

Notes

_____

_____

_____

_____

_____

_____

_____

_____

_____

_____

_____

_____

_____

Something About the Name
You Shall Call Upon

There's something about the name you shall call upon
When you're hurting, low in heart, and you have fallen,
Asking for forgiveness for all you have done;
Repentance from your heart is where your life has begun.

Now in spirit and truth, the enemy is knocking at your door;
The enemy knocking at your spiritual core
To see if he again can hurt you, and cause you to fall;
You remember that holy name you are supposed to call upon.

That name ... in that name redemption is there;
That name ... in that name where you cast all cares;
That name ... that holy name that you call when you fall;
Jesus is that name you shall call upon.

God is the Reason

God Almighty is greater than any and all things,
He's the reason why we praise and sing.
He's the reason why we are alive,
He's the reason why we do strive.
He's the reason why we can see,
He's the reason why we do achieve.
He's the reason why we can hear,
He's the reason why we are sincere.
He's the reason why we can smell,
He's the reason why we can tell.
He's the reason why we can taste,
He's the reason why we don't make haste;
On him we do wait.
He's the reason why we sense a touch,
Thank you, God Almighty, for loving us so much.

Walking with God's Spirit

As long as you walk, talk, and live by God's word
He will continue to dwell within your body's core
Your body is God's temple
And living for him does not come simple

Trials and tribulations
Make you walk stronger with Jesus Christ
Remember, the word of God says
Weeping only endureth for a night

This is the new day.
So give praise, glory, and honor to God for the light
Because walking, talking, and living by God's Spirit
Is what is right.

What My Lord Will Do ...

He comforts me through all my trials,
Whether they be short or for a while.
He heals all sicknesses and diseases too;
Since he did it for me, I know he'll do it for you.
He is the greatest known sacrifice
By dying for mankind to have an abundant life.
"Touch not mine anointed, and do my prophets no harm."
The passage is found in Psalm 105:15; all have been warned.
Thinking of going against what the Lord's words say?
Watch out because the wrath of God will soon be on its way.
What my Lord will do for his own ...
He protects them as parents over children they nurtured and honed.

That's what my Lord will do.

AUTHOR'S KNOWLEDGE

&

Where the author obtained the knowledge of God's will...

Where Does the Author's Knowledge Comes From?

❧

Hebrew 10:25, Ephesians 4:11-13, II Timothy 2:15, Luke 18:1; 1Thessalonians 5:17; Matthew 21:22, II Timothy 2:1-2; Galatians 5:22-23, Leviticus 19:18, I John 4:7, Matthew 5:44, I John 4:8 & 16, Numbers 23:19, Psalm 119:104

The Author's knowledge comes from the following.

- Sunday school
- testimonies of others
- life experiences
- doctrinal training received in the House of God
- reading and studying the Holy Bible
- praying unto God
- teaching the Word of God
- being a witness of God
- showing love and compassion for God's people

Notes

_____

_____

_____

_____

_____

_____

_____

_____

Message to Sinners and Believers

God is good; God is great
God is Love; he's not fake

If you're wondering how I know
The Holy Bible tells me so
And I feel him deep within my soul

God is almighty; his presence is everywhere
He's all knowing; he's always there

If you're wondering how I know
God's word and training told me so
And I feel him deep within my soul

God is holy peace; an awesome provider
The ultimate healer; undefeatable warrior

If you're wondering how I know
Being a doer of his will acknowledges me so
And his Holy Spirit that's deep within my soul

If you want to obtain what I know
And feel God within your soul
Then repent, be baptized, and be blessed with the Holy Ghost

Oh wait … it does not stop there
You must show compassion and that you really care

About others' souls; not just your own
You must do God's will, or the Holy Ghost will go

Once it leaves, you become an empty vessel
And all you do will be in vain
Because your heart wasn't right
In him you truly can't proclaim

Bearing false witness … you're not in God's will
You must start all over, and begin to till

Just like preparing the ground for growth of what is planted
You must till that soul you helped keep dismantled

Should the person not receive the words God gave
Kick off the dust and be on your way

Now God will intervene
He heard what you have said and has seen
That you have done all that you can
In truth to tell of his great plan

God will judge those who choose not to hear or take heed
He will bring forth correction so that they will see
That he is above all and controls everything
So let's watch ourselves and be who God would have us to be

READER'S THOUGHTS

The following pages are area to take more notes or record your personal thoughts.

NOTES/PERSONAL THOUGHTS

_____

_____

_____

_____

_____

_____

_____

_____

_____

_____

_____

_____

_____

_____

_____

_____

_____

_____

_____

_____

_____

_____